Come to My Party!

by Emilie Barnes

Illustrations by Michal Sparks

THREE RIVERS PUBLIC LIBRARY
25207 W. CHANNON DRIVE
P.O. BOX 300
CHANNAHON, IL 60410-0300

D1317015

HARVEST HOUSE PUBLISHERS
Eugene, Oregon

Come to My Party!

Text Copyright © 2001 by Emilie Barnes
Published by Harvest House Publishers
Eugene, OR 97402

All works of art reproduced in this book are copyrighted by Michal Sparks and may not be reproduced without the artist's permission. For more information regarding art featured in this book, please contact:

Mr. Gifford Bowne
Indigo Gate
1 Pegasus Drive
Colts Neck, NJ 07722
(732) 577-9333

Design and Production: Garborg Design Works, Minneapolis, Minnesota

Library of Congress Cataloging-in-Publication Data
Barnes, Emilie.
  Come to my party! / Emilie Barnes ; illustrations by Michal Sparks.
    p. cm.
  ISBN 0-7369-0552-9
    1. Entertaining—Juvenile literature. 2. Parties—Juvenile literature. 3. Cookery—Juvenile literature.
[1. Parties. 2. Cookery. 3. Party decorations. 4. Handicraft.] 1. Sparks, Michal, ill. II. Title.

TXT731 .B357 2001
793.2'1—dc21   00-066982

Some material in this book has previously appeared in:
    Let's Have a Tea Party by Emilie Barnes with Sue Junker (Harvest House Publishers, 1997)
    Cooking Up Fun in the Kitchen by Emilie Barnes with Anne Christian Buchanan
    (Harvest House Publishers, 2000)
    The Very Best Christmas Ever by Emilie Barnes with Anne and Elizabeth Buchanan
    (Harvest House Publishers, 1998)
    My Best Friends and Me by Emilie Barnes with Anne Christian Buchanan (Harvest
    House Publishers, 1999)
    15 Minute Family Traditions & Memories by Emilie Barnes (Harvest House Publishers, 1995)

All rights reserved. No part of this publication may be reproduced, stored in a retrieval system, or transmitted in any form or by any means—electronic, mechanical, digital, photocopy, recording, or any other—except for brief quotations in printed reviews, without the prior permission of the publisher.

Printed in Hong Kong
    01 02 03 04 05 06 07 08 09 10 / NG / 10 9 8 7 6 5 4 3 2 1

Contents

Let's Have a Party!

Hello, my name is Emilie Marie! I'm so excited you're here because I'd like you to come to my party—actually, let's make that parties.

I just returned home from visiting my Aunt Evelyn's house, which is one of my favorite places to go. Aunt Evelyn loves to have fun and she likes to do nice things for people, so she has a lot of parties. Some of them are big parties, like the formal tea she had this weekend for her friend Yoli's birthday. I was the only guest there who wasn't a grown-up, but I had a great time. In fact, Aunt Evelyn's best friends remind me a lot of grown-up versions of my own best friends! Some of Aunt Evelyn's

parties are not big at all, like the picnic she fixed for just the two of us. It only took a few minutes for her to make the sandwiches and gather together some cookies and fruit, but it was a special time together for just us—and that's what makes a party.

I was so excited when I got back home that I called up my best friends. (We're all in a friendship club, The Angels, and we love to have fun times together.) Some of them weren't home, so I sent them e-mail messages and typed in "Come to my party!" for the subject heading. Of course, they all wrote back right away.

You're invited to our first party, too. It's a planning party to plan parties! Does that make sense? We're going to share all of our

ideas and talk about the kind of parties we want to have. Christine told
me she wants to have a Victorian tea
party like the one at Aunt Evelyn's
that I told her about. Maria loves the
beach and wants to have a Tropical
Beach Party. (Now all we need is
sunny weather!) Elizabeth loves to
read, so she has a great idea for a
Bookworm Tea Party.

Jasmine, who is adopted,
is just getting to
know some of her
extended family
members.

She wants to have a
party with friends *and*
family. Then Aleesha e-
mailed me with a really
wonderful party idea. It's
called a "Helping Hands"
party, and we'll do things at
the party to help people who
are in need.

Elizabeth thought it might be
nice to invite other friends to our
parties besides the Angels, maybe a
girl who is new in school or a
younger sister who usually doesn't
play with us. We all thought that was
a very good idea.

I have a big yellow pad of paper
with all sorts of party ideas written
down on it. The Angels might have to
have a party once a month (or more!)
with all of the creative things we've
thought up.

So come to my party—and then
get ready for some parties of your
own!

1 A Proper Victorian Tea

When I told Christine about Aunt Evelyn's formal Victorian tea party, she started sighing and said, "Oh, I wish I could have been there!" about forty times. I wish she could have been there, too! Christine's favorite things are roses and princesses and anything romantic. She would have loved the elegant dresses the ladies wore, the flowers that made the house seem like a scene right out of one of our favorite books, *The Secret Garden*, and the classical music that was playing in the background. (Aunt Evelyn hired a string quartet; Aleesha has some classical piano CDs that we have our eye on for this party!)

We're going to have our Victorian tea party in the spring, and some of our moms are going to help us with the food and decorations. (That's a good idea for any party.) But we're going to do most of it ourselves, and each of us is going to invite someone we'd like to get to know better. A few of the Angels are inviting new girls at school. I'm inviting Aleesha's little sister, Marti!

Delightful Decorations

• **A Victorian Table**—If you have one, you can use a pretty white cloth made out of linen or crisp cotton for this fancy tea party. You can also use matching white linen or cotton napkins. Silver napkin rings look really elegant (Christine's mom has some of those), but you might want to tie satin ribbons around the napkins instead. They look pretty and colorful. Large gold or silver doilies make beautiful placemats. Then, for the centerpiece, you might use a fresh bouquet of roses and greenery. (Aunt Evelyn used daisies and baby's breath for hers.) Pretty serving pieces like china plates, silver trays, and Grandma's teapot or cut-glass punchbowl are very special touches.

• **Hats for the Ladies**—Decorate straw hats with silk flowers and beautiful ribbons. Wear your hats for tea—and be sure to pose for an elegant group picture!

Cucumber Tea Sandwiches

cucumbers (how many cucumbers
    depends on how many people
    you will be serving)
white bread
whipped cream cheese
unsalted butter, softened
salt

1. Peel the cucumbers and slice them very thin. Sprinkle the slices with salt and then put them on paper towels to drain.

2. For each sandwich, spread a little bit of cream cheese on two slices of bread. Then layer the cucumber slices on one piece of bread, but don't stack them higher than 1/4 inch.

Menu
Cucumber Sandwiches
Pretty Petit Fours
Chocolate-Dipped Strawberries
Assorted Herbal Teas with Cream
and Sugar

3. Cut them into square tea sandwiches. You can cut them into squares, triangles, long strips, or fun shapes. Tea sandwiches are easier to cut if you chill them first. Wrap your sandwiches in a slightly damp kitchen towel and then in waxed paper before you put them in the refrigerator. When you're ready to serve them (and with an adult watching), trim the crusts with a serrated knife (the kind of knife that has teeth). Then cut the sandwiches into shapes. You can use that same knife, but sometimes I like to use cookie cutters to make special shapes.

7

Pretty Petit Fours

an already-cooked pound cake
2 cups powdered sugar (or more if you
*   make a lot of little cakes)*
6 tablespoons water
food coloring
tubes of decorating gel or, if you want,
*   edible flowers*

1. Cut the pound cake into one-inch slices. Trim the crust from each slice and then cut each slice into four squares.

2. To make the icing, add water—a tablespoon at a time—to the powdered sugar. Mix the sugar and water well after each table-spoon you pour in. Then add a couple drops of food coloring (red or yellow) and stir the icing until it is very smooth. You don't want any lumps!

3. Place the small cake squares on a wire rack (the kind you use for cooling cakes and cookies) and drizzle some icing over each one. Be sure that each little piece of cake is thoroughly cov-ered. (Make more icing if you need to.) Then let the icing dry.

4. Once the icing is dry, decorate your petit fours with gel or edible flowers.

Chocolate-Dipped Strawberries

whole fresh strawberries,
*   washed and dried*
semisweet chocolate chips

1. Fill a small deep container (like a coffee cup) with chocolate chips and place it in the microwave. To melt the chocolate, heat it on high for 20 seconds, open the microwave and stir the chocolate, and then heat it again for 20 more seconds. Continue heating the choco-late at 20-second intervals until it is just melted.

2. Hold a strawberry by its broad top and dip the bottom part of the berry into the melted chocolate. Set the strawberry on waxed paper to cool. Continue dipping until you've dipped all the strawberries. Store the dipped berries in the refrigerator.

Something Fun to Make

- **Do-It-Yourself China**—At a discount or thrift store, buy plain white or glass plates. Give one to each of your guests and then have everyone use glass or china paints (you can get them at craft stores) and tiny paintbrushes to decorate their plates with a sweet design.

Fun & Games

- **Broken Cups**—Before the party, draw a pretty teacup for each guest. Make sure to include on each cup a special message like "Thanks for being my friend!" or "I'm so glad you came." Then cut each drawing into eight or ten pieces that aren't too easy to put back together. Put the pieces of each drawing into pretty envelopes (one set of teacup pieces per envelope) and give an envelope to each guest as she arrives. Then, sometime during the party, have your guests assemble their cups ("On your mark, get set, go!"). The first one who puts her broken cup back together is the winner.

- **Teatime Memory Teaser**—Bring out a tray on which you have put a number of well-known tea objects like a teacup, teabags, a tea strainer, a sugar bowl, milk, a lemon, and baked goodies. Let your guests look at it for a full minute. Then take the tray away and give each person a pencil, a piece of paper, and three minutes to write down everything she saw on the tray. Remember, the more items you put on the tray, the more you tease the memory! Have a special gift ready for the person who remembers the greatest number of objects. You could let that person choose something from the tray.

9

2 Great Generations Gala

Jasmine was the mastermind behind this wonderful party. (Don't you just love the word "gala"?) We were talking about girls our own age who we'd like to invite to our parties when Jasmine said, "Wait a minute, Emilie Marie. Weren't you the youngest at Aunt Evelyn's tea party?" I was the *youngest*—by a lot! But it was so much fun. The ladies were all so kind to me, and I loved listening to all of their stories.

So then we started talking about how we love to listen to our moms and grammies tell stories about when they were little girls and about all the neat things we learn from them. That's when Jasmine came up with the idea for this party. She's adopted and her family recently moved to this area, so she's just getting to know some of her relatives who live close by. Maria doesn't have a grandmother close by, but she has an "adopted grandma" at church who she's going to invite.

I'm going to invite my two best friends in the whole world—my mom and my grammy.

Delightful Decorations

- **A Cozy Table**—Cover your table with a family quilt. Make a centerpiece out of framed family photos or other family treasures. You could even display family scrapbooks on a side table.

- **Forget-Me-Not Napkin Rings**—Forget-me-nots are beautiful blue flowers that grow on delicate thin stalks, and those stems make them perfect for shaping into little wreaths! Find some silk forget-me-nots at a craft store. You'll need several stalks for each napkin ring. Hold three or four stalks together and make a circle out of them. Then use floral wire to hold the wreath together. For a sweet touch, hide a handwritten note between the napkins and the ring. A message of love like "No one could ever take your place" would be perfect.

Menu

Nutty-Raisin Tea Sandwiches

Grammy's Old-Fashioned Scones with Sue's Crème Fraiche or Mock Devonshire Cream

Heirloom Treasures

Hot Spiced Tea

Nutty-Raisin Tea Sandwiches

raisin bread
soft butter
whipped cream cheese
chopped pecans

1. For each sandwich, spread two slices of raisin bread with a little bit of butter. Then spread on some cream cheese.

2. Sprinkle chopped pecans on top of the cream cheese and close the sandwich. Cut off the crusts and then use small cookie cutters to cut your sandwiches into fancy shapes.

Grammy's Old-Fashioned Scones

2 cups flour
1 tablespoon baking powder
2 tablespoons sugar
1/2 teaspoon salt
6 tablespoons butter
1/2 cup buttermilk
1 lightly beaten egg

1. Mix together all the dry ingredients. Then use a pastry cutter or two knives to cut in the butter until the mixture resembles coarse cornmeal. (Grammy will know how to do that!) Make a well in the center of your dough and pour in the buttermilk. Stir until the dough clings together and is a bit sticky. (You don't want the scones to be tough.)

2. Put the dough on a floured surface and flatten it into a circle that's 1 1/2 inches thick and between 6 and 8 inches across. Working quickly, cut the dough into triangles like pieces of a pie or use a large round biscuit cutter to cut it into circles.

3. Put your triangles or circles on an ungreased cookie sheet. Make sure that the sides of the scones don't touch each other. Then brush some of the lightly beaten egg on top so that your scones will be a shiny, beautiful brown.

4. Bake at 425 degrees for 10 to 20 minutes until the pastries are light brown. Serve your scones with some special cream (you'll find two recipes following, but in a pinch you can buy whipped topping at the store) or your favorite preserves and jams (red raspberry or strawberry are nice).

Sue's Crème Fraiche

1 cup heavy cream
1 tablespoon buttermilk

1. Pour the cream and the buttermilk into a saucepan and stir them together on your stove. Have the burner set at a medium heat. Heat the mixture just until the chill is off (that's about 90 degrees if you have a kitchen thermometer).

2. Once the chill is off, pour the mixture into a glass jar, cover it lightly with a piece of wax paper, and let it sit in a warm place (65 to 70 degrees) to thicken. It takes between 12 and 20 hours.

3. Once it's thick, replace the wax paper with plastic wrap or a tight-fitting lid and refrigerate your crème fraiche for at least 6 hours. (It will last for about two weeks if you keep it in the refrigerator.) You might want to whip your crème to make it thicker or add a little sugar to make it sweet.

Mock Devonshire Cream
(makes 1 1/2 cups)

1/2 cup heavy cream or 8 ounces
of softened cream cheese
2 tablespoons confectioners sugar
1/2 cup sour cream

1. In a chilled bowl, beat the cream until medium-stiff peaks form. Add the sugar during the last few minutes of beating. (If you use cream cheese, just stir it and the sugar together.)

2. Fold (that's a gentler movement than stirring) in the sour cream and blend.

Heirloom Treasures

dried apricots
white melting chocolate
    (from the baking section
    at the grocery store)
small silver baking cups
cooking spray

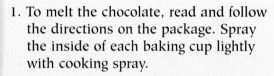

1. To melt the chocolate, read and follow the directions on the package. Spray the inside of each baking cup lightly with cooking spray.

2. Dip half of each apricot in chocolate. Swirl each apricot around so it gets a nice, thick coating of chocolate. Place each dipped apricot—chocolate side down—in a silver baking cup. Refrigerate your yummy treasures.

Hot Spiced Tea

1 cup dry instant tea
    (I like decaffeinated)
2 cups dry powdered orange drink
3 cups sugar
1/2 cup red hots
1 teaspoon of ground cinnamon
1/2 teaspoon powdered cloves
1 package (about 1 cup)
    lemonade mix

Stir together all of the ingredients and place the mixture in a covered container. When it's time to make the tea, use one heaping tablespoon for each cup of hot water. Stir it well and then enjoy.

Something Fun to Make

- **Jazzy Jewelry**—These earrings are so easy to make and really fun to wear! Cut two same-sized shapes (hearts, stars, flowers, squares) from cardboard. Using acrylic paint or nail polish, paint both sides of the shapes. (You can also cut out pictures from magazines and glue them to the cardboard.) Coat the cardboard shapes or pictures with clear varnish and allow them to dry completely. Glue each shape to an earring base (available at craft or hobby shops). Then wear your pretty creations.

Fun & Games

- **Interview Time**—To learn more about your mom or grammy (or special friend) and what her life has been like, ask! Before your party, write down some questions you would like an older family member to answer and some stories you'd like her to tell. You could, for instance, ask her to describe all the different houses she has lived in or tell you about her best friend when she was little. Ask about a very happy time in her life and a very sad time. Find out what she dreamed about being when she was a little girl and what she wanted to be when she grew up. Ask her, too, about what have been the most pleasant surprises in her life. When you finish, let her interview you.

- **Family Pictures**—Look at family photo albums together and talk about the pictures. Turn this fun into a treasure hunt by looking for things like the strangest clothes, the worst hairstyle, the cutest baby, and the most adorable guy. Choose your own interesting things to find!

3 | Helping Hands Angel Party

Our friendship club is called The Angels, and do you know what angels do? They help people. So when Aleesha gave us the idea for this "Helping Hands" party, we all looked at each other and smiled and said, "Of course!"

This is a helping project that's fun to do *with* your friends—not just *for* them—and it can really help you be a friend to someone who is in need.

All you need to do is have a party. Decide on a theme (Aleesha, who loves sports and has a pool, suggested an Olympics theme), make invitations, and invite everyone in your class or group. Then plan and decorate and get ready for one of the most fun parties anyone ever had. In the summer, it could be a swimming party and a barbecue. In the fall or winter, it could be a harvest celebration or a Christmas bash. It's just like any other party, except for two things:

One, it should be the liveliest, most fun party of the year...

And two, everybody is supposed to bring something. It's like bringing presents to a birthday party except you've told them what to bring...and the presents aren't for you! They're for somebody in your community who could really use a friend and a helping hand.

Delightful Decorations

- **"Can-Do"**—This is a quick and easy way to decorate—and your guests will provide the decorations as they arrive! Just tie some colorful ribbons and streamers to empty boxes, baskets, or bags with handles. Add some balloons, too. Then have your guests bring cans of food for the local food bank. As they arrive with the cans, you'll fill up your displays—and be ready to deliver them. You can also collect cans or paper to recycle. Save the money and give it to a local food bank or children's shelter.

- **"Let It Snow"**—This is the same idea as the Can-Do party, only with a different theme. Have everyone bring coats and hats and gloves for the homeless shelter. Toys and books and clothes could go to a children's home. Just be sure to tell everybody on the invitation what you plan to do with the stuff they bring. You might be surprised at how much there is. When you give them a chance, most people really like to be angel friends—helping friends!

Chicken-Pecan Angels

white and wheat bread slices
3 boneless, skinless chicken breasts,
  cooked and chopped coarsely
1/2 cup finely chopped pecans
1/4 cup finely chopped celery
1/2 cup mayonnaise
butter

Menu
Chicken-Pecan Angels
Angel Food Cake with
Strawberries and Cream
Pink Lemonade or Hot Chocolate
(depending on the season)

1. Butter bread slices.

2. Mix chicken, pecans, celery, and mayonnaise.

3. Make sandwiches, using about 3 table-spoons of the pecan mixture on each sandwich.

4. Chill sandwiches, then use cookie cutters to cut into angel shapes. Wrap in waxed paper until ready to use.

17

Angel Food Cake with Strawberries and Cream

1 angel food cake (purchased or
   homemade)
2 pints fresh strawberries
1/4 cup sugar
1 container whipped topping

1. Wash the strawberries. Cut off the green stem and leaves. Then slice the strawberries. Sprinkle them with sugar and set them aside.

2. With a long knife (and an adult's help), slice the cake horizontally twice so that you have three layers.

3. Brush the loose crumbs off each layer and place the bottom layer on a pretty plate. Spread the top of the layer with whipped topping and then cover it with strawberry slices.

4. Place the second layer on top of the bottom one. Spread the top of this layer with whipped topping and strawberry slices.

5. Place the top layer on the cake and frost the top with the rest of the whipped topping. Decorate the cake with the strawberries you have left. Store the cake in the refrigerator until it's time for tea.

Something Fun to Make

• **Because-You're-Special Boxes**—This is a fun thing to make because it makes you feel so good when you give it away! A little box is all you need to get started. I found a little paper-mache box at the craft store that's shaped like a heart. (It's about six inches long.) Use decoupage glue and a brush to cover it with cutouts from pretty wrapping paper, and paint the inside of the box a matching color. You can even use a gold paint pen to write "Because You're Special" on the front of the box. Then tuck something special in the box—some candy, a little toy, a few coins—and give it away to somebody just because!

Fun & Games

• **Helping Hands**—You need a big T-shirt or sweatshirt to do this one. Two people put on the T-shirt! One puts her head through the neck hole. The other person stands behind her (under the shirt) and puts her arms through the arm holes. From the front, you see one bulky person with one person's head and another person's arms. This double person is now going to act out a story or a poem. It's easiest if you have somebody else tell the story. The people inside the shirt have to work together to make a face and hand gestures such as smiling, frowning, pointing, scratching, etc. This will be even funnier if you use a table of props—like a glass of water, some food, makeup, etc. Watch what happens when the "hands" try to bring the glass to the "head"!

• **The "Know Your Friends" Show**—Here's a fun way to find out just how well you know your friends! All you have to do is write down a bunch of questions (like "What is your favorite singer or music group?" or "Who is your favorite teacher" or "If you could travel anywhere in the world today, where would you go?") onto little slips of paper. Then fold each question in half and place in a wide-mouthed jar or hat. Then you're ready to play.

You need at least three people for this "game show"—a "host" and at least two "contestants." The host draws the question and reads it out loud. The contestants write down their answers. Then each contestant tries to guess what the *other* person's answer was. Every right guess earns a point. After ten questions, add up the points and see who knows each other better. Now try another set of contestants, or let the host try. The person with the most points wins.

4 Summer Bugs in the Garden Party

Right before school ended last spring, Elizabeth and Maria studied bugs in science. They started to get really into bugs and before we knew it all of the Angels were buggy about bugs! Not creepy, crawly bugs—cute bugs, like ladybugs (my favorite!) and june bugs and happy yellow bumblebees. Maria even got a set of bug sheets and pillowcases for her bed! (Her room is decorated with a lot of paper flowers, so the bugs felt right at home.)

The garden in our backyard is one of my favorite places to be—and a favorite place for bugs to be, too. I love to lie on my back in the soft, cool grass and watch the fluffy clouds float by, smell the sweet air, and listen to the wind dance with the leaves. The roses and gladiola are always so pretty. And the little table out there is a nice place to read a book, sit and think, visit with a friend, and have a Summer Bugs in the Garden Party.

20

Delightful Decorations

- **An Outside Table**—Cover a picnic table or patio table with a bright flowered sheet or a colorful tablecloth. A table with an umbrella can be especially pretty. You can decorate edges of the umbrella with garlands of ivy and wind a vine around the pole. If you don't have a table, spread out a picnic blanket and set your "table" on the ground. Use beautiful things from your garden as you decorate. Freshly picked flowers tucked in a watering can make a wonderful centerpiece. Use your imagination and have fun!

- **Garden Napkin Rings**—Cut napkin rings from cardboard tubes and then cover them with flowery fabric or contact paper. Use white napkins or give each guest a napkin that matches the flowers in her garden placemat.

Bug Bites

plain round cookies—like sugar cookies or gingersnaps—for the bug bodies
tubes of colored icing
small candies like red hots or mini M&Ms for spots, eyes, etc.
licorice or fruit-flavored candy strings for legs, antennae, etc.

Use the icing and candies to turn cookies into a plateful of bugs to serve your guests. Don't forget the ants! Or save the fun to share with your friends. Make or buy the cookies ahead of time and have your guests help you turn them into bugs.

Menu
Bug Bites
Garden Patch Cupcakes
Assorted Seasonal Fruit
Lemonade

RIVERS PUBLIC LIBRARY
25207 W. CHANNON DRIVE
P.O. BOX 300
CHANNAHON, IL 60410-0300

Garden Patch Cupcakes

one chocolate cupcake for each guest
chocolate frosting
crumbled chocolate sandwich
    cookies
mint leaves
thin drinking straws
edible flowers or artificial
    flowers

Frost each cupcake with chocolate frosting. Then sprinkle each one with crumbled cookies to make dirt for your garden. Next cut the straws into 2- or 3-inch pieces and stand one in the middle of each cupcake. Then place a flower, stem down, into each straw. If you use edible flowers, let your guests know that it's okay to eat the blossoms.

Something Fun to Make

• **Painted Flowerpots**—Carefully wash 3 1/2-inch clay pots (one for each guest plus one for you!) and let them dry. At the party, give your guests acrylic craft paints and brushes to decorate their pots, some newspapers to work on, and old T-shirts to wear during the fun. Plan to paint the flowerpots at the beginning of the tea so they can dry during the rest of the party. When your guests leave, be sure each one has a plastic bag of potting soil and a small packet of seeds. It will be a great reminder of your special bugs in the garden party!

22

Fun & Games

• **Pin the Bee on the Blossom—**
Paint a big piece of poster board with a very large rose. Draw winding stems, rosebuds, and leaves around the edges. Then, using a black marker, draw five or six bees onto yellow papers from self-stick pads. Make sure that at least part of the bee is on the sticky part! Then cut out the bees. At the party, blindfold each guest with a mask made of flowery material and have them take turns trying to stick the bee onto the large rose.

• **Start Your Own Garden—**This is a fun activity that you get to keep working on! My grandfather has a big garden, and the Angels love to help him with it. This year, Papa Bob even helped us start our own Friends Garden in Maria's backyard! We each chose something to grow in it: tomatoes for Maria, pink impatiens for Christine, corn for Aleesha, sugar peas for Jasmine, and pansies for me, plus a big pumpkin patch back by the fence for Elizabeth. We had a great time planting it and a great time taking care of it—even weeding was fun when we did it all together. Best of all, we can plan another party to pick tomatoes and corn and peas and beautiful flowers…and enough plump orange pumpkins to decorate all of our porches and make six yummy pumpkin pies!

5 Wish-it-Were-Sunny Decorator Party

Last summer the Angels had big plans for a tropical beach party. We gathered up all of our beach supplies—swimsuits and sunglasses and sunscreen and beach towels and radios and a whole bunch of equipment to build great big sand castles—and we even packed some sunny sandwiches and fruity smoothies and our favorite soft drinks in a big cooler. Maria's family has a van, so her mom was all set to drive us to the beach. Christine's mom was there, too.

So there we all were, in our tropical-print tops and skirts and flip-flops, loading stuff into Maria's van, when it started to rain. And then it started to pour. We went inside and turned on the weather channel—big storms all day, the weather forecaster said—and that was the end of our tropical beach party. Well, you can imagine how bummed we were! That's when

Christine's mom, who is an interior decorator, said, "We might not be able to go to the beach, but we can bring the beach to us!" So we got out a bunch of art supplies and turned Maria's living room into a tropical paradise. Then we had our moms drop off our raingear so we could have some outdoor fun, too. It turned out to be one of our favorite parties ever!

- **Bright Lights**—Maria's living room has a bunch of tall potted plants. We got out her Christmas boxes and wound brightly colored lights all around the plants. Combined with our tropical clothes, it really made the room shine!

- **Paradise Pictures**—Big rolls of colored paper really come in handy. You can make almost anything with them! You can buy them by the foot in craft stores. We used yellow paper to make a big sun and taped it to the ceiling. Then we used green and brown paper to make a bunch of palm trees and taped them to the walls and bookcases. (Make sure you use tape that doesn't leave marks or sticky stuff behind when you remove it, and never put tape on anything valuable. We asked Maria's mom for permission before we put up the decorations.) We also decorated the table with some seashells from Maria's collection in her room. Now all we needed was a coconut!

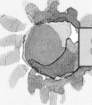

Sunny Sandwiches

sandwich bread
apricot jam or orange marmalade
carrot slices
raisins

For each sandwich, spread two slices of bread with apricot jam. Cut off the crusts and use a biscuit cutter or round cookie cutter to cut the sandwiches into circles. Use carrot slices to make the rays of the sun. Add raisins for eyes and a sunny smile.

Menu
Sunny Sandwiches
Fruit Dippers
Fruity Smoothies

Nut 'n Honey Dip

1/3 cup peanut butter
1/3 cup honey
1/4 teaspoon cinnamon

Just mix all the ingredients together in a bowl. This dip is great for apples, pears, and carrot sticks. Or try spreading it on bread and eating as a sandwich.

Sweet Cream Dip

1 8-ounce packaged lowfat
   cream cheese
1/3 cup undiluted apple juice
   or orange juice concentrate
pinch of cinnamon
2-3 tablespoons chopped pecans
   (if you like them)

Put the cream cheese in a bowl and mash it with a fork until it's smooth. Stir in juice, nuts, and cinnamon and stir until combined. Try this one with pineapple chunks, strawberries, bananas, and grapes.

Fruit Dippers

It's fun to dip chunks of fruit into a creamy sweet sauce. We've given you three yummy dips to choose from— and you can use your favorite fruit to dip. This recipe makes as much as you want to make.

2-3 cups of your favorite fruit, including:
- sliced banana
- oranges, peeled and pulled into sections
- cantaloupe or honeydew melon, cut in chunks
- fresh or canned pineapple, cut in chunks
- green or red seedless grapes, pulled into little bunches of two or three
- apples or pears, cut in chunks
- whole strawberries with their green hulls left on
- maraschino cherries with stems left on
- 1/2 cup lemon, orange, or pineapple juice
- fruit dip of your choice

1. Put bananas, apples, or pears in the large bowl and toss with the juice. This will help keep them from turning brown.

2. Arrange the fruit on a plate so that it looks pretty.

3. Use toothpicks or your fingers to pick up the food, dip it in your favorite sauce, and eat.

Easy Chocolate-Berry Dip

1 can prepared chocolate frosting
1/2 jar raspberry or strawberry jam

1. Spoon frosting and jam together in the bowl or cup.

2. Microwave on high about 3 to 4 minutes or until the jam is dissolved, stopping the microwave every minute to stir.

3. When the frosting and jam are completely mixed, put the bowl into the refrigerator and chill it. This dip is great with berries and cherries—or try dipping vanilla cookies or angel food cake chunks.

bananas, pineapples, or peaches. (My favorite is frozen strawberries and bananas!) Cut the fruit into chunks if it's big and add it to the blender a few pieces at a time. Frozen fruit will take longer to blend in, but it makes a cool, rich smoothie!

3. When the fruit is all blended in, add honey or sugar and blend until the smoothie is sweet enough for you. Be sure the blender stops completely before you reach in to taste!

Fruity Smoothies

1 1/2 cups of lowfat vanilla yogurt
1/2 cup of milk
2 cups of your favorite fresh,
    frozen, or canned fruit

1. Mix together yogurt and milk in a blender.

2. Turn the blender on high and carefully add about 2 cups of fresh, frozen, or canned fruit—such as strawberries,

Something Fun to Make

• **Ice Cream Cone Cupcakes**—These are fun to make *and* fun to eat. You can get really fancy with your decorations. We had Christine's mom make one for a sample, and she had such a great time that she decorated six or seven of them! You will need:

> 1 box of cake mix
> flat-bottomed ice cream cones
> 1 can of frosting
> decorations—chopped nuts, sprinkles, small candies, maraschino cherries (whatever you like!)

1. Follow the directions on a box of cake mix to make a smooth batter and pre-heat the oven to 350 degrees.

2. Instead of pouring the batter into cake pans, pour it into flat-bottomed ice cream cones. Fill each cone up to about 1 inch from the top. Put the filled cones on a cookie sheet or muffin pan and bake them in the preheated oven for about 30 minutes.

3. Let your cake-cones cool completely, then spread the tops with canned frosting. Decorate with chopped nuts, sprinkles, small candies—or even a cherry on top!

• **Tropical Balloon Toss**—We put on our raincoats and went outside for this one. This game carries the anticipation that the next toss will cover someone with water! You play with a partner. Have the partners line up facing each other, about six or seven feet apart. Give each team one water balloon. At the starter's command, the person holding the balloon will toss the balloon in an under-hand motion for her partner to catch. If the balloon breaks, the team is eliminated from the game. If not, the partners stay in the game. (If the balloon hits the ground but does not break, the partners are still in the game.) The starter will give directions for those remaining to step back one giant step. Again, the person makes an underhand toss of the bal-loon. Those who have balloons intact will continue playing the game until one set of partners is left in the game with an unbroken balloon.

30

• **Pop Bottle Fill**—This is another good outdoor game! You play this one with a partner, too. You'll need pop bottles of the same size, a large bucket of water, and paper cups. Place the large bucket of water in the center of a circle of players who are lying on their backs on the grass with their feet pointing away from the bucket of water and their heads about six feet from the water bucket. The players, while lying down, place pop bottles on their foreheads. The lying down players' partners are given paper cups. The object is to have them run to the bucket of water, fill their cups with water, hurry to their partner's pop bottle, and try to empty their cups into the bottle. As you can imagine, the players lying down will get soaked! Of course, the prize goes to the team that fills the pop bottle first.

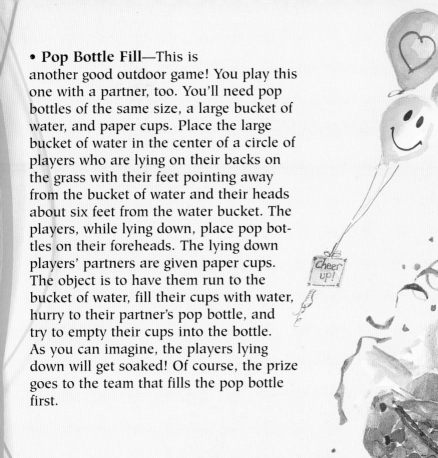

Cheer up!

6 | A Stars and Stripes Soiree

"Oh, say can you seeeee!"

Oops! I'm just practicing singing "The Star-Spangled Banner" for the Fourth of July. (Some of those high notes are really hard to hit!) I love all of the parades and potlucks and fireworks on the Fourth. It's a day that just seems made for a party.

Most of the Angels already have lots of Fourth of July family traditions. Jasmine's family rents a beach cabin for the weekend. Elizabeth's neighbors always have a block party complete with fireworks and a parade. Maria is often out of town spending the Fourth with her cousins who live in another state. We always have a big family picnic, and this year my parents gave me permission to invite some friends whose families don't have big Fourth of July plans.

Now, I'd better get back to practicing those high notes!

Delightful Decorations

• **Tambourine Napkin Rings**—Oh, say can you see these fun table decorations! First cut cardboard tubes into rings and paint them black or silver (or red, white, and blue). You can also put gold or silver stars on them. Then use a hole punch to make four holes on both edges of each ring. Lace a thin black ribbon (about 6 inches long) through each hole and use it to tie jingle bells to the napkin rings. Then slide a red, white, or blue napkin through each tambourine.

32

- **Strike-Up-the-Band Placemats**—Your guests will sing for their supper with these fun placemats! You will need:

> white construction paper
> a ruler
> a pencil
> a black marker
> someone who knows how to read music

Draw a large musical staff (five horizontal and parallel lines) on each piece of white construction paper. Then set each guest's name to music. My placemat might look like this:

EM-I-LIE MA-RIE

Menu

Pasta Salad
Flag Cake
Blueberries
Strawberry Lemonade

Pasta Salad (8 servings)

1 pound thin spaghetti
1 8-ounce bottle Italian salad dressing
2 3/4-ounce jars Salad Supreme salad seasoning
2 chopped celery stalks
1 chopped green pepper
1 thinly sliced onion
1 pint cherry tomatoes
1 6-ounce can ripe pitted olives

1. Cook spaghetti according to package directions. Drain and rinse in cold water.

2. Combine spaghetti, salad dressing, and salad seasoning.

3. Add celery, green pepper, and onion.

4. Chill 3 to 4 hours.

5. Just before serving, add tomatoes and olives.

Flag Cake

1 white cake mix
1 cup heavy cream
1 tablespoon sugar
1/2 teaspoon vanilla
1/2 cup fresh blueberries
2 cups sliced fresh strawberries

1. Mix and bake cake according to package directions in 9" x 13" baking dish.

2. Place cake on attractive serving dish or platter.

3. Beat cream until soft peaks form. Add sugar and vanilla.

4. Spread whipped cream in an even layer over top of cake.

5. Place 2 lines of blueberries at right angles in top left corner to form a 4-inch square. Fill square with additional lines of blueberries. Leave small amount of white cream showing between the berries.

6. Use overlapping sliced strawberries to form horizontal red stripes from side to side on cake, allowing cream to show for white stripes.

7. Refrigerate cake until serving time.

Something Fun to Make

• **Here Comes the Parade!**—Think of this as a traveling kind of craft project! Gather up pots and pans, tambourines, horns, and toy instruments. You can carry flags and even tie colored balloons on your bikes. Wear red, white, and blue clothes and march and ride around the neighborhood, asking others to join in the parade.

Fun & Games

• **Sing-a-Long Time**—The Fourth of July is a great day for singing! Patriotic songs, folk songs, your current favorites—all are perfect for a group sing-a-long. You can ask someone to play the guitar or piano or sing along with a CD. You might even rent a karaoke machine.

• **Guess Who's Humming**—Ask your guests to stand in a circle. The person who is "It" stands blindfolded in the center. As your friends walk slowly around "It," they sing a song. When "It" says, "Stop!" the people in the circle stop moving, but they keep singing. "It" then points to one of the guests, and everyone else immediately stops singing. The person to whom "It" pointed starts to hum the song, and "It" tries to guess who is humming. If "It" guesses correctly, she and the one humming trade places. If "It" doesn't guess who was humming, she tries again. Let each of your friends have a chance to be "It." (This game works best if your guests know each other pretty well.)

1 | A Fall Campout Party

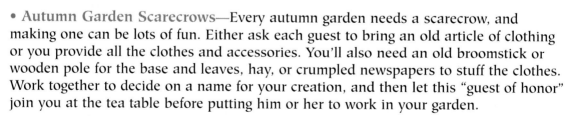

Have you ever climbed a mountain? Well, Aleesha's dad has climbed a lot of them! He's even tried to reach the top of Mt. McKinley in Alaska. He had to turn around because of a snowstorm, but he almost made it to the top. This fall he plans to lead us on a hike up a mountain close to where we live. We aren't going to have to do anything fancy like rock climbing or fixing ropes (that's a mountain-climbing term we learned from Aleesha's dad), but we *are* going to have a party to celebrate finishing our hike! If the weather is good, we might even make it an outdoor campout.

I'd better get going—Christine is here on her bike. We're going for a long ride to get in training for our outdoor adventure!

Delightful Decorations

• **Autumn Garden Scarecrows**—Every autumn garden needs a scarecrow, and making one can be lots of fun. Either ask each guest to bring an old article of clothing or you provide all the clothes and accessories. You'll also need an old broomstick or wooden pole for the base and leaves, hay, or crumpled newspapers to stuff the clothes. Work together to decide on a name for your creation, and then let this "guest of honor" join you at the tea table before putting him or her to work in your garden.

• **Trail Mix-and-Match Table Toppers**—Trail mix is a good source of energy for hikes and other strenuous activities. You can buy it, but it's fun to mix your own from ingredients you like best. The recipe makes as much as you want to make! Just mix up an assortment for your guests, put some mix in individual bags, and tie the bags shut with pretty ribbon in fall colors.

> roasted, unsalted nuts (peanuts, walnuts, pecans, almonds, mixed nuts)
> dried fruits (apples, apricots, raisins, dates, pineapple, cranberries)
> toasted seeds (sesame seeds, sunflower seeds, pumpkin seeds)
> extras (candy-coated chocolate candies, cereal)

Put every ingredient you've collected into a different bowl. Then add handfuls from the small bowls into the big one, creating the kind of mixture you want. Pack your trail mix in plastic bags for the road.

Make-Your-Own Ranch Dressing or Dip

Menu
Cool Veggies with Ranch Dip
High-Energy Snack Balls
Grammie's Spiced Cider

If ranch is your favorite dressing, it's easy to make your own! To make a ranch dip, just use sour cream instead of buttermilk. You'll make about 2 cups of dressing or dip.

1 cup mayonnaise or lowfat mayonnaise
1 cup buttermilk (for dressing) or lowfat sour cream (for dip)
2 tablespoons onion powder
1 tablespoon dried parsley flakes
1/4 teaspoon garlic powder
1/4 teaspoon salt
1/4 teaspoon black pepper

Put all the ingredients in a bowl or jar. (The dip is easier to make in a bowl.) Stir or shake until all the ingredients are blended together. Chill in the refrigerator before serving.

High-Energy Snack Balls

1 cup granola
1/2 cup unsalted sunflower seeds
2 tablespoons toasted wheat germ
1/2 cup raisins
1 one-ounce package hot cocoa mix
3/4 cup crunchy peanut butter
1/2 cup honey
1 cup shredded coconut

1. Mix granola, seeds, wheat germ, raisins, and cocoa mix.

2. Add peanut butter and honey, then mix some more.

3. Shape into balls and roll in coconut.

Grammie's Spiced Cider

This is really easy!

2 quarts of apple cider
1/4 cup of brown sugar, packed tightly in the cup
1 teaspoon whole allspice
1 teaspoon whole cloves
2 cinnamon sticks
1/2 lemon, thinly sliced

1. Put all ingredients together in a pan.

2. Heat on the stove, stirring until the sugar melts. When the cider is hot, serve it in mugs.

Fun & Games

• **Fall Nature Walk**—Go on a nature walk and collect interesting rocks, sticks, leaves, etc. Make a collage out of the neat things you found.

• **Press Flowers**—Press flowers or leaves in a book. When dry, use to make note cards, bookmarks, and pictures. (You can also press an assortment of flowers ahead of time and make crafts with them at your party.)

Something Fun to Make

• **Cool Veggies**—Did you know that you can decorate with veggies? Just a few cutting tricks will make pretty vegetable shapes.

Cucumber wheels. Use a vegetable peeler to peel long stripes on the sides of a cucumber. Then slice the cucumber into wheels about 1/2 inch thick. The wheels will have a pretty striped edge.

Carrot curls. Use a vegetable peeler to peel a large, fat carrot. Then use the peeler to peel off big strips of carrot. Drop the strips into ice water and watch them curl up.

Celery brushes. Cut the celery into pieces about 4 inches long. Then make a lot of little cuts about 2 inches long down one end of the celery. Drop the pieces of celery into ice water and the cut end will fan out into little brushes.

Radish flowers. Cut the roots off the radish and hold it upright, with the root end down. Now carefully slice the top of the radish—don't cut all the way through to the stem end. You can make "roses" and "chrysanthemums" this way. Drop the radish into the ice water to open up into flowers.

Tomato roses. With a paring knife, carefully remove the peel of a medium-size tomato. Start at the top and cut around and around so the peel comes off in one piece. Then arrange the peel into a rose shape.

8 | A Back-to-School Bash

I absolutely love summer! I have so much fun going to the swimming pool, having sleepovers with my friends, going to the beach, and reading fun books. But every year it seems like summer is over way too soon. And even though I like learning new things in school and making new friends and getting to know my teacher, I'm always a little—okay, a lot—sad when summer is over. It always seems like summer just all of a sudden ends with fading memories of fun times and a big rush to get ready for school.

Then I had the idea for this Back-to-School Bash. It would be a little of summer—a sleepover party with lots of yummy food and goofy games—and a little of fall—school-theme decorations and a fun back-to-school craft project. Then we could get up in the morning (by the way, sleeping in is definitely allowed at this party!) and fix ourselves a big breakfast, look through our pictures of summer activities, plan our back-to-school outfits, and maybe even help each other start loading up our book bags!

Delightful Decorations

- **School Supplies**—Decorate the table with back-to-school supplies—pens and pencils, crayons and notebook paper, binders and rulers. When the party's over, you have your supplies ready for the first day of school!

- **Breakfast Trays**—Put your breakfast treats on trays and treat your friends to breakfast in bed (or breakfast in sleeping bag)! Put a pretty cloth or placemat on the bottom of a large tray. Add china, glasses, flatware, and a colorful napkin tied with a ribbon. A little vase filled with flowers adds a special touch, too—try using an old pill bottle and a single daisy or rosebud.

Menu
Homemade Apple Pancakes
Crunchy Potato Casserole
Breakfast Biscuits
Fresh-Squeezed Orange Juice

Homemade Apple Pancakes

2 eggs
1 1/2 cups buttermilk
3 tablespoons butter, melted
1 1/2 cups flour
1 tablespoon sugar
1 1/2 teaspoons baking powder
1/2 teaspoon baking soda
1/2 teaspoon salt
1 tablespoon lemon juice
2 apples, peeled and grated

1. Heat a skillet or griddle over medium heat.

2. Use a medium-size bowl and an electric beater (if you have one; if not, you can use the old-fash-ioned way of a fork or a wire whisk), and beat the eggs until they are well blended.

3. Add the buttermilk, melted butter, flour, sugar, baking powder, baking soda, salt, and lemon juice and beat until the mixture is smooth.

4. Add the grated apple and stir with a spoon until the batter is well blended.

5. Have an adult test the skillet or griddle to check that it is hot enough.

When it is hot enough, spray the griddle surface with a light coat of non-stick cooking spray.

6. Using a large spoon or a 1/4-cup measure, pour the batter onto the hot surface. As each pancake spreads, it should be about 4 inches in diameter. Be careful to keep the pancakes from touching one another.

7. When the pancakes are puffy and full of bubbles, they are ready to be turned over. Once they are turned, cook them for a few more minutes or until they are nicely browned. Serve with butter and syrup. (Serves 4)

Crunchy Potato Casserole

2 pounds frozen hash browns
1 can cream of chicken soup
8 ounces sour cream
10 ounces grated sharp cheese
1/2 cup chopped onions
dash of salt and pepper
2 cups corn flakes
1/2 cup melted margarine or butter

1. Mix the above ingredients together and put in a 9" x 13" casserole.

2. Top with corn flakes (crushed) and melted butter or margarine.

3. Bake uncovered at 375 degrees for 45 minutes. This freezes well.

Breakfast Biscuits

2 cups whole-wheat pastry flour or
*   white flour*
2 1/2 teaspoons baking powder
1/2 teaspoon baking soda
1/2 teaspoon salt
1 cup buttermilk
3 tablespoons oil (extra virgin olive oil
*   preferred)*

1. Preheat oven to 425 degrees.

2. In a medium bowl, blend the flour, baking powder, baking soda, and salt.

3. In a 2-cup measure or small bowl, whisk together the buttermilk and oil.

4. Stir liquid ingredients into dry ingredients just until mixed; beat 10 strokes.

5. Drop spoonfuls of dough on ungreased cookie sheet.

6. Bake at 425 degrees for 12 to 15 minutes until lightly golden on the bottom. (Makes 10 biscuits)

Something Fun to Make

• **A Welcome Basket**—This is a fun way to welcome someone to your town or school and start making friends with her. Find a large basket (an old Easter basket will do fine) and line it with a piece of pretty cloth. Then fill the basket with fun things to help the new girl feel welcome and at home. Here are some ideas:

- decorated pencils, erasers, etc.
- list of fun places to go in town
- snacks—trail mix, cookies, sugarless gum, etc.
- information about sports clubs, craft classes, etc.
- commercial coupons for local ice cream shops, pizza, etc.
- homemade coupons for things to do with you and your family—like go skating, come over for dinner, help wash your dog, and so on
- stamps or note paper for writing friends back home
- tiny rubber stamps and an ink pad
- an easy-to-grow plant
- a stuffed animal with a big bow
- something special from your part of the country—a sun pillow from Arizona, a sheriff's star from Texas, wild rice from Minnesota, a country music CD from Nashville, a hat or pennant from the local college or professional team.

• **Giggle Belly**—Everybody lies on their backs in a circle with each person's head on the next person's stomach. Pretty funny already, huh? But the game hasn't even started! Choose someone to begin. She says "HA!" If she says it good and loud, the head on her stomach will bounce! That person is next. She has to say "HA HA." The next person says "HA HA HA"—and continue all around the circle until somebody loses track of how many "HA HAs" she has or you're all laughing so hard you can't go on.

• **Marshmallow Gobble**—Wear old clothes for this one. Tie a string around the middle of a big marshmallow and dip it in chocolate sauce. Hang the string from a tree branch or the ceiling. Blindfold the first person, spin her around, then have her try to catch the marshmallow in her teeth and nibble it off the string. No hands! If she succeeds in thirty seconds, she gets a prize. Then it's somebody else's turn.

9 Bookworm Tea Party

All of the Angels like to read, but Elizabeth definitely wins the bookworm award! Her room is covered with books. She tries to keep them on her bookshelves, but she reads very fast and soon there are books on the bed, books on the desk, books on the floor, books...well, you get the picture! Elizabeth and I share a favorite book, *Little Women*. We love the characters in that book, especially Jo. And one of our favorite parts of the book is the Christmas scene where the girls, despite not having very much money, give their mother a very special gift.

Well, Elizabeth and I were at her house reading and talking (surrounded by a huge pile of books, of course!) when she came up with the idea of having a Bookworm Tea Party. We decided that this definitely needed to be a cozy indoor party. And then we decided that it would be perfect to have it during the holidays when her house was all decorated for Christmas. Now Elizabeth is reading books about having her book party. The party is months away, but she's already decided that we are to come dressed as our favorite book character and that we need to bring our favorite book. What a bookworm!

Delightful Decorations

- **Cozy Reading Nook**—Set up a corner of the room with big pillows, little pillows, and an assortment of warm blankets. This can be your reading nook! You can also make your own pretty pillows out of worn old pillows that no one uses anymore. Just use fabric glue to attach a pretty dishtowel or napkin to the front of the pillow. Another neat thing to do is to glue a crocheted doily onto a solid-color pillow for a pretty, old-fashioned look.

- **Lending Library**—Clear space on a counter for your very own lending library. Have your guests bring some of their favorite books to the party (ones they aren't currently reading; make sure they are marked with the owners' names). When all the guests have arrived, set up the books on the table and let your friends "check out" each other's books. Have a notebook and pen handy to record who's borrowing which title.

Cinnamon Minis

These little baby cinnamon rolls are really cute. The best part about them is that you can make just a few for a snack or a whole bunch for a party. This recipe makes 60 Cinnamon Minis.

1 package refrigerated biscuit dough
(the kind that comes in a round
can in the dairy case)
1 stick butter, softened
3 tablespoons cinnamon
3 tablespoons sugar
a little flour for rolling the dough
i/2 cup powdered sugar
for icing
water

Menu
Cinnamon Minis
Spicy Party Mix
Bookworm Cupcakes
Mexican Hot Chocolate

1. Preheat the oven to 400 degrees. Sprinkle a little flour on the surface where you're going to roll the biscuits and on the rolling pin. Tear off a sheet of wax paper and put it on another counter.

2. Now open the can of refrigerated biscuit dough and take out one of the biscuits. Put it on the rolling surface and roll it flat with the rolling pin. Don't worry if it rolls around the pin; just peel it off. Pretty soon you'll have a flat, oval pancake.

3. When the biscuit is pretty flat, pick it up and stretch it with your fingers until it's a rectangle instead of an oval—sort of pull at the corners. You want a rectangle about the size of a 3 x 5 index card. Put it down on the wax paper and spread it thickly with softened butter.

4. Mix the cinnamon and granulated sugar together in a bowl. With a spoon, carefully spoon some of this mixture onto the flattened-out biscuit. Try to sprinkle it evenly and thickly and cover the whole biscuit up to the edge.

5. Start at one of the short edges of the biscuit rectangle and carefully roll it up into a sausage shape. Lay it down on the wax paper with the "seam" down and gently stretch it with your fingers to make it a little longer and skinnier. Then use a sharp knife to cut the "sausage" into 6 pieces. Pick them up with your fingers and put them around the edge of an ungreased cake pan, sides touching. Don't worry if one of them "unwinds"; just roll it back up again.

6. If you want a Cinnamon Mini snack, you can go ahead and bake these six now. If you're cooking for a crowd, repeat steps 2-5 until you've used up all the biscuits. You will fill the whole of one cake pan and maybe part of another. Let them touch, but don't crowd them.

7. Bake your pan of Cinnamon Minis for about 8 minutes, until they are puffed up and golden brown. Take them from the oven and put them on a heatproof surface to cool while you make the icing.

8. To make Cinnamon Mini icing, put 1/2 cup powdered sugar in a small bowl. Add a few teaspoons of water and stir with a wire whisk. Add more water a little at a time, stirring after every addition, until you have a thick white frosting. (It doesn't take much water!) When the icing is mixed, use a knife to dot a little on every warm Cinnamon Mini. Let the icing set, then use a spatula to remove them from the pan to a serving tray—or to your mouth!

Bookworm Cupcakes

one cupcake for every guest
frosting
gummy worms

1. Frost your cupcakes.

2. Put gummy worms on the top of each cupcake. Now they're bookworm cup-cakes!

Spicy Party Mix

5 cups of your favorite cereals and/or snack crackers
1/3 cup of melted butter
4 teaspoons of Worcestershire or soy sauce
3 teaspoons of flavored salt—like onion, garlic, and celery salt

1. Mix together about 5 cups of different ingredients—like wheat or corn squares, oat "o"s, pretzels, or even chow-mein noodles.

2. Mix together the butter, Worcestershire or soy sauce, and flavored salt.

3. Stir everything together and spread out in jelly roll pans or roaster pans. Bake at 350 degrees for an hour, stirring every 10 minutes.

Mexican Hot Chocolate

2 tablets Mexican chocolate (This is chocolate combined with sugar, almond, and cinnamon. You can probably find it in the "ethnic" section of a large grocery store or a Mexican market.)
1/4 cup water
2 quarts milk
whipped cream
cinnamon
hand beater or molinillo

1. Gently melt chocolate tablets in the water over very low heat.

2. Add the milk, then heat, stirring, until just under the boiling point.

3. Remove chocolate from heat and pour it into a jug or pitcher. Beat with the molinillo or a hand beater until foamy.

4. Serve topped with whipped cream and a dash of cinnamon.

Note: If you can't find the Mexican chocolate, use four 1-ounce squares of unsweetened chocolate. Before you beat the chocolate, add 2/3 cup sugar, 1/4 teaspoon ground cinnamon, and 2 teaspoons of almond extract.

Something Fun to Make

• **Secret Treasure Journal**—Give each of your guests 16 sheets of lined paper (the kind with the holes) and three pieces of pretty ribbon. Tie the ribbon through the holes to make a secret treasure journal. Then let your friends decorate the cover with stickers, stamps, and marking pens. Each of your friends will now have her own special book to write dreams and memories in.

My Journal

• **Book Trade**—This is the next chapter of the lending library game! Have each guest bring a favorite book to the party. Give everyone a chance to tell why they brought their book. If you want, and if your guests know each other well enough, encourage them to trade books for a few weeks. Make sure people who trade books know who is borrowing theirs and when they will get it back. It's a good idea to have the owner of the book write her name, her phone number, and the date she's expecting it back on the inside front cover. Book owners may also want to have those who borrow their books sign their name and date on the inside back cover. You and your friends might even decide to make a certain day each month "Book Trading Day." It might be fun to see which book has the most signatures at the end of the year.

• **Write a Poem!**—Do you like to write poems? I do. Here's a kind of poem that's fun and easy to write for a special friend. Just write her name in capital letters up and down on a sheet of paper. The letters should be on top of each other, in a straight line. Then, for every letter, write a word or phrase that starts with that letter and describes your friend. When you've finished writing the poem, copy it neatly on a nice piece of paper and give it to your friend. Here's a word poem I wrote for Christine:

Creative
Happy
Ready for fun
Independent
Sweet
Trustworthy
Ideas are everywhere!
Never mean
Emilie Marie's friend!

THREE RIVERS PUBLIC LIBRARY
25207 W. CHANNON DRIVE
P.O. BOX 300
CHANNAHON, IL 60410-0300

10 A Pink and White Heart Party

She's my best friend and very sweet, so it's only fitting that Christine was born on Valentine's Day. Every year Christine and her mom plan her birthday party and they do a really great job. One year we had a very elegant high tea, another year we had a teddy bear party, and when we were younger we had a Winnie-the-Pooh party that was lots of fun.

Well, this year I came up with the great idea to have a surprise party for Christine! So I called her mom (when I knew that Christine would be at her piano teacher's house) and we planned the theme (pink and white hearts), the decorations, the food, and everything. All of the Angels are getting together to work on the party. Maria is making the bonbons. Jasmine and Elizabeth are making the decorations. Aleesha is in charge of the games. And I'm helping with more food and organizing things.

Christine will be at her piano lesson for an hour on the day of the party, so that will give us just enough time to get things set up. I can't wait to see her look of surprise when she walks in the door!

• **Pink and White Peppermint Carnations**—To make these pretty flowers, you will need:

> red and white tissue paper cut into lots of 3" x 3" squares
> florist's wire or long green pipe cleaners
> green florist's tape

Make a stack of five squares of tissue, alternating red and white. Fold the stack back and forth like a fan, then pinch the folded stack in the middle and wrap a piece of wire around it, twisting the wire together below the paper to make a stem. With scissors, cut a row of little notches into each end of the folded stack. Then, one by one, pull apart the individual squares of tissue paper to form petals. Fluff out the petals to finish your flower. To decorate Christine's birthday table, we made a bunch of these carnations. We also made some plain red and white ones. We twisted red and white crepe paper streamers together and draped them around the edge of the table, holding them to the edge of the tablecloth with pins. Then we taped a few of our carnations over the pins to hide them.

• **Have a Heart**—Jasmine and Elizabeth, the decorating committee, cut out tons of pink and white construction paper hearts. They put these hearts everywhere—on the front door, taped to the walls. They even had heart garlands strung across the room. Then they bought a bunch of heart confetti and sprinkled it all over the birthday table.

Pink and White Snowballs

vanilla ice cream
strawberry or peppermint ice cream
flaked coconut

1. Line a small cookie sheet with wax paper.

2. Using an ice cream scoop, make two ice cream balls—one vanilla and one strawberry or peppermint—for each guest.

3. Roll each ball in coconut. Place the balls on the cookie sheet, cover the cookie sheet with foil, and freeze the snowballs until they are very firm.

Menu

Pink and White Snowballs
Cherry Bonbons
Have-a-Heart Dessert
Raspberry Tea

Cherry Bonbons

maraschino cherries with stems
semisweet chocolate chips

1. Take the cherries out of the jar they came in and put them on paper towels so the liquid can drain off.

2. Fill a small deep container (like a coffee cup) with chocolate chips and place it in the microwave. To melt the chocolate, heat it on high for 20 seconds, open the microwave and stir the chocolate, and then heat it again for 20 more seconds. Continue heating the chocolate at 20-second intervals until it is just melted.

3. Hold the cherries by their stems and dip them in chocolate. Set the dipped cherries on waxed paper. Chill these bonbons in the refrigerator.

Have-a-Heart Dessert

*graham crackers
ice cream or frozen yogurt
red cake decorating gel*

Our delicious, no-bake Valentine's Day dessert "box" is made of graham crackers—and the "gift" inside is your family's or friend's favorite ice cream or frozen yogurt!

1. Top a graham cracker square with a scoop of ice cream or frozen yogurt as high and wide as the graham cracker.

2. Place four graham crackers on the sides of the ice cream and press lightly, forming a square. Top with another cracker.

3. Create a "ribbon" and "bow" with a tube of red cake decorating gel. Freeze until ready to serve.

Raspberry Tea

*a pot of tea, any flavor (raspberry would be yummy!)
fresh raspberries, 3-5 for each cup of tea*

Brew your tea. Put raspberries in each cup before pouring the tea.

Something Fun to Make

• **Hair, Hair!**—Make a heart-shaped hair ornament by twisting a red pipe cleaner into a heart. Wrap red or white lace ribbon around it and glue on some glitter. When the glue has dried, attach the heart to a barrette or hair clip.

Fun & Games

• **Valentine Treasure Hunt**—Buy a package of inexpensive valentines or make your own. Then write a different note on each of 10 to 15 cards, or write one word per card to form a message. Hide the cards throughout the room (or throughout the whole house—or even take the party outside if the weather's nice!). Give a written clue on the outside of each envelope directing your friends to the next card. Include small treats for your guests with the last valentine.

• **Balloon Walk**—Inflate a number of pink and white balloons and draw hearts on each with a felt-tip pen. Divide the group into two or more equal-size teams. At the signal, each person must carry the balloon between her knees to the goal line and back. If the balloon breaks, she must come back for a new one and start over. The first team to finish is the winner. A large balloon for each team member makes a cute prize. You can also play this game as an individual competition, using a stopwatch to time each competitor. The one with the shortest time is the winner. Or you can set up an obstacle course for players to walk through on their way to the goal line.

The Heart of Partytime Manners

"It's time for a party!" Those are words I'm always happy to hear. Sometimes I'm the party-giver.

And sometimes I'm a partygoer. Either way, parties are fun. Partytime manners are not really hard to learn. Mostly they're just everyday good manners and mealtime manners and visiting manners combined with an extra spark—making sure everyone has a special good time.

Making Party Plans

If I want to give a party of my own, the first thing I need to do is to check with my parents and maybe some other adults. I need their permission and their help! We need to talk together about what kind of party it will be, where it will be held, and how many people I can invite.

Once those things have been decided, I can start planning. I really like this part of being a party-giver.

First, I need to think about party food and decorations and activities. Then I need to decide who to invite. Sometimes I like to have a very small party with just two or three friends.

Other times I invite a bigger group. I think it's fun to invite people I know from different places and help them get to know each other, too.

If my party is going to be small, I usually just invite a few of my good friends. If it's big, I try to invite all of one group of people—my whole Brownie troop or all of the girls in my class. That way, people's feelings don't get hurt by being left out.

Please Come

If my party is going to be very casual, like a sleep-over with a few friends, I usually just call them on the phone and invite them—or sometimes my mom calls their mother.

For a bigger or fancier party, though, it's better to send out written invitations. These can be plain or fancy, cute or serious, and I can make them by hand or fill in the "blanks" on ready-printed invitations. I usually like to make my own because it's fun. I fold a piece of construction paper, cut it in a fancy shape without cutting through the fold, decorate the outside, and then write the invitation on the inside.

For example, when I gave a special garden tea party for five of my friends, I cut out little invitations in flower shapes and wrote this on the inside:

Please come to a special
garden tea party
on Saturday,
the fourteenth of June
at 2 p.m.
at Emilie Marie Barnes' house
2838 Rumsey Drive
Please wear Sunday clothes and a pretty hat.

RSVP 682-4714

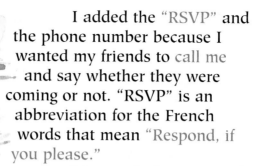

I added the "RSVP" and the phone number because I wanted my friends to call me and say whether they were coming or not. "RSVP" is an abbreviation for the French words that mean "Respond, if you please."

It's usually best to send the invitations through the mail. I can also pass them out by hand if I am absolutely certain that someone won't see someone else get an invitation and feel left out.

When it's time to have the party, Mom and Dad and I (and the Angels if we're throwing the party as a group) always work together to make the food and put up the decorations. (I help them when they have parties, too.) And of course I pitch in to get the house looking nice and clean.

It's Partytime!

When the time for my party finally rolls around, sometimes I feel nervous. Aunt Evelyn says it's all right to feel